50 Relaxing

MANDALAS

ADULT COLORING BOOK

50 Relaxing
MANDALAS
ADULT COLORING BOOK

50 Relaxing

MANDALAS

ADULT COLORING BOOK

50 Relaxing
MANDALAS
ADULT COLORING BOOK

50 Relaxing
MANDALAS

ADULT COLORING BOOK

50 Relaxing
MANDALAS

Adults Coloring Book

50 Relaxing

50 Relaxing
MANDALAS

ADULT COLORING BOOK

50 Relaxing

MANDALAS

A ADULT COLORING BOOK

50 Relaxing

MANDALAS

ADULT COLORING BOOK

50 Relaxing

MANDALAS

ADULT COLORING BOOK

50 Relaxing
MANDALAS
COLORING BOOK

50 Relaxing

MANDALAS

ADULT COLORING BOOK

50 Relaxing
MANDALAS

ADULT COLORING BOOK

50 Relaxing

MANDALAS

ADULT COLORING BOOK

50 Relaxing
MANDALAS
ADULT COLORING BOOK

50 Relaxing
MANDALAS

ADULT COLORING BOOK

50 Relaxing
MANDALAS
THE COLORING BOOK

50 Relaxing

MANDALAS

ADULT COLORING BOOK

50 Relaxing

MANDALAS

ADULT COLORING BOOK

50 Relaxing
MANDALAS
AN ADULT COLORING BOOK

50 Relaxing

MANDALAS

ADULT COLORING BOOK

50 Relaxing
MANDALAS
ADULT COLORING BOOK

50 Relaxing
MANDALAS
ADULT COLORING BOOK

50 Relaxing
MANDALAS
ADULT COLORING BOOK

50 Relaxing

MANDALAS

50 Relaxing

MANDALAS

ADULT COLORING BOOK

50 Relaxing
MANDALAS
ADULT COLORING BOOK

50 Relaxing
MANDALAS
ADULT COLORING BOOK

50 Relaxing
MANDALAS

ADULT COLORING BOOK

50 Relaxing

MANDALAS

ADULT COLORING BOOK

50 Relaxing
MANDALAS

ADULT COLORING BOOK

50 Relaxing
MANDALAS

ADULT COLORING BOOK

50 Relaxing

MANDALAS

AN ADULT COLORING BOOK

50 Relaxing
MANDALAS

A ADULT COLORING BOOK

50 Relaxing

MANDALAS

AN ADULT COLORING BOOK

50 Relaxing
MANDALAS

50 Relaxing
MANDALAS

ADULT COLORING BOOK

50 Relaxing
MANDALAS
ADULT COLORING BOOK

50 Relaxing
MANDALAS
ADULT COLORING BOOK

50 Relaxing

MANDALAS

Adult Coloring Book

50 Relaxing
MANDALAS
ADULT COLORING BOOK

50 Relaxing

MANDALAS

50 Relaxing

MANDALAS

ADULT COLORING BOOK

50 Relaxing

MANDALAS

50 Relaxing
MANDALAS
ADULT COLORING BOOK

50 Relaxing

MANDALAS

Made in the USA
Thornton, CO
05/12/24 00:52:08

236090e8-1247-4e1b-a68e-6aa04dacf4efR01